Jude James was born in south-west Hampshire. He was educated at Reading and Portsmouth Universities, specialising in local and regional history. In 1996 he was elected a Fellow of the Society of Antiquaries. For well over thirty years Jude James has made a detailed study of the economic and social history of the Wessex region and has written and lectured extensively on many aspects of the region's history.

He is the author of several books ranging from a detailed analysis of life in the New Forest in the early nineteenth century (*Comyn's New Forest*, 1982) to an edition for the Dorset Record Society of a farmer's diary for the year 1758 ('The Diary of James Warne' in *Farming in Dorset*, 1993). Most recently he has had published *East Boldre: A New Forest Squatters' Settlement 1700-1900* and *'The Children of the New Forest' and its Author.* Amongst his other books are: *Wimborne Minster: The History of a Country Town* (1982) and *Hurst Castle: an Illustrated History* (1986).

He is a past president of the Hampshire Field Club and Archaeological Society, chairman of the Lymington and District Historical Society, and a member of the editorial board of *The Hatcher Review* (a journal specialising in Wessex history and literature).

*Following page*
A group of pupils with their mistress outside
the National 'Minster' School in King Street, Wimborne,
taken about the turn of the century.

DISCOVER DORSET

# THE VICTORIANS

JUDE JAMES

THE DOVECOTE PRESS

The almshouses at Trent founded by Mrs Mary Turner,
wife of the rector, in 1846. They represent the strong and
practical sense of charity towards the 'deserving' poor that
was a hall-mark of the Victorian Christian ethos.

First published in 1998 by The Dovecote Press Ltd
Stanbridge, Wimborne, Dorset BH21 4JD

ISBN 1 874336 60 1

© Jude James 1998

Jude James has asserted his rights under the Copyright, Designs
and Patent Act 1988 to be identified as author of this work

Series designed by Humphrey Stone

Typeset in Sabon by The Typesetting Bureau
Wimborne, Dorset
Printed and bound by Baskerville Press, Salisbury, Wiltshire

A CIP catalogue record for this book is available
from the British Library

1 3 5 7 9 8 6 4 2

# CONTENTS

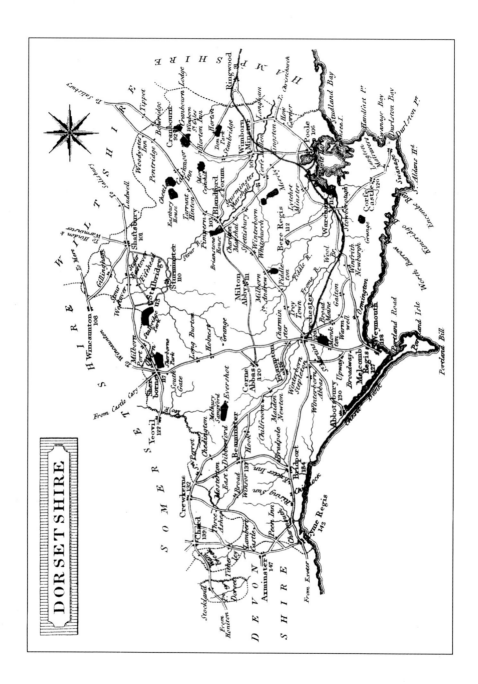

# DORSETSHIRE

# PROLOGUE

William Barnes, the renowned Dorset dialect poet, was 36 years old when Queen Victoria came to the throne in 1837 as a young woman of eighteen. Neither could then have guessed at the changes and upheavals that were to mark her long sixty-three years reign. But in his later years Barnes reflected:

> *Ah! naïghbour John, since I an' you*
> *Wer youngsters, ev'ry thing is new.*

Throughout Victoria's reign Dorset remained a rural county, although its economic life continued to be based on agriculture, the old methods and traditions were to undergo a fundamental shift with the introduction of new crops, mechanisation and the steam engine. The old open commonfields which still survived in some parishes into the late 1830s were all to disappear under the impact of parliamentary enclosure, with the sole (and odd) exception of Portland.

In keeping with national trends, the population slowly but inexorably rose, so that the 159,385 recorded in the census of 1831 was to increase to over 200,000 by 1901. But more significant was the fact that, even in an agrarian county, the rural parish populations decreased from their mid-century peaks whilst those of the larger towns increased.

A traveller arriving in Dorset in 1840 would have found the system

Map of Dorsetshire.
This map shows the main turnpike roads of the mid-nineteenth century, yet omits the Wimborne to Puddletown road of 1841. Note the mileage distances from London recorded for all the principal places. The route of the Southampton and Dorchester Railway, opened in 1847, is shown between Ringwood and the Dorchester terminus. In 1896 the detached part of Dorset, beyond the western county boundary, was moved into Devonshire whilst the Wambrook projection was transferred to Somerset.

of parochially maintained roads dominating communications, whilst a few turnpiked roads served the routes to and between the main towns. Had he arrived in 1901 it would almost certainly have been by rail and the roads would then have been no more than gravelled tracks linking the villages and connecting them to the nearest railway station. It is true that the first motor vehicles made their appearance before the nineteenth century ended, but not in sufficient numbers to have any impact.

In the general election of July 1837 the restricted electorate of Dorset sent 14 members to the Commons, eleven of whom represented the towns. By 1901, with a much wider franchise, established under the Reform Act of 1884 which for the first time included agricultural workers, the county was represented by four members only, none of whom now solely represented the towns.

Administration changed markedly. At the outset the county was governed at a local level by appointed justices of the peace acting in pairs in small matters, but who came together four times a year in peripatetic quarter sessions to undertake both the judicial and administrative functions of the county. By 1888 an elective county council was in control and a mere six years later the parish councils were created to bring democratic governance down to the smallest unit. Policing, which in the early decades of the nineteenth century was carried out by constables, either elected by the rural manor courts or by the corporations in the boroughs, became a unified county service in 1857. The new force was divided into nine areas corresponding to the existing petty sessional divisions and, in each area, brick-built police stations were constructed, a few surviving to the present day.

The Poor Law Amendment Act had been passed in 1834, drastically changing a system that had operated for more than two centuries, and its provisions were being felt in Dorset with the creation of unions of parishes and new workhouses being built. These were at Beaminster (now private flats), Bridport (now an infirmary), Cerne Abbas (now private flats), Dorchester (now a hospital), Poole (demolished), Shaftesbury (demolished), Sherborne (demolished), Sturminster Newton (partially demolished), Wareham (now an infirmary) and Weymouth (now a hospital). At Blandford

The former police station at Blandford remains the last of those that can be clearly seen in the original state. They stood in every Dorset market town and were all of a similar pattern, comprising red brick with slate roofs and limestone dressings. They were built in the late 1850s.

Typical of the workhouse 'Bastilles', erected after the passing of the Poor Law Amendment Act in 1834, Sturminster Newton provided a good example of the plain uncompromising design which ensured segregation of sexes in two splayed wings.

and Wimborne (both demolished) the old workhouses were adapted to the new requirements. The high costs of providing for the poor in the earlier part of the nineteenth century were mitigated under the new regime but at a social cost so unacceptable that, within a decade or two, a considerable easing of the severe conditions at first laid down for the workhouses under the principle known as 'less eligibility', meaning conditions in the institution were to be less good than the worse outside.

Even schooling underwent major changes as the ad hoc system, lacking any form of uniform curriculum or compulsion, was transformed into a state school system, though continuing to draw heavily on, and co-operating with, the many Church of England National Schools. The national system had to provide board schools in places where there was no denominational school or where the existing provision was inadequate.

The changes in religious worship were, perhaps, less remarkable but many medieval parish churches were refurbished, modernised or completely rebuilt in the sixty years of Victoria's reign. In the

Outside the Beaminster Union Workhouse, young inmates parade before the camera in their distinctive garb. Drums are borne by two of the youngsters while others have fifes, suggesting this may have been at the beginning or conclusion of a church parade.

Bournemouth was only added to the county of Dorset in 1974 but long before that its economic and social impact on the eastern part of the county was immense. Bournemouth only received its charter of incorporation in 1856 but thereafter grew spectacularly. This view, looking west from East Cliff, shows the burgeoning town nestling in the Bourne valley with its magnificent pier. The wide south-facing sandy beaches and equable climate ensured its growth as a high class and major resort in Victorian times.

growing towns' new churches, such as St John's at Weymouth, were built to provide for the increased population. Methodism certainly continued to flourish in the countryside and a number of new chapels were erected for worship.

The enthusiasm for sea-bathing which had characterised outdoor leisure activity in the late eighteenth century became ever more popular in the nineteenth and was to transform towns such as Weymouth, Swanage and Bournemouth (only added to Dorset in 1974).

The fortunes of other towns were more variable. Poole, which had enjoyed a heyday with its Newfoundland trade in the eighteenth century, fell into the doldrums. Its harbour facilities, lacking a direct railway connection, meant it could not compete with Southampton – revealed by the fact that only 64 ships used Poole in 1847. Even the Thursday market declined and the fish market was largely deserted. But a revival of fortunes started in the late 1870s with the growth of Bournemouth. The constructional demands of the new resort meant that imported timber was vital and Poole proved to be the best

This engraving of Poole harbour shows it being revitalised as trade picked up after the lull of the first half of the nineteenth century. The demand for timber for building purposes was an important element in bringing new maritime trade.

harbour for this purpose. Also slate, much in demand for roofing, was shipped in large quantities from north Wales. By 1900 the Poole and District Electric Traction Company had established the first tramways.

With the perceived (but probably unrealistic) threats from France, Portland was selected as one of the south coast naval bases, necessitating the construction of large breakwaters to enclose what had been Portland Roads. Massive forts were constructed on the Verne and at the Nothe at Weymouth to protect the fleet. The breakwater was constructed with convict labour and a huge prison was built on Portland to accommodate those employed on this great piece of civil engineering.

# FARMING AND RURAL LIFE

It is against the backcloth of agrarian life that we can best view Dorset farming and the activities related to it; despite the changes already inferred, it continued to form the county's economic base as well as providing the ethos for most of its people. When Victoria ascended the throne most of her Dorset subjects lived in its villages, and they continued to do so at the time of her death some 63 years later, despite depopulation and the growth of towns.

Mechanisation had already begun to have an impact on the number of workers needed on farms and this was a process that was to both continue and to accelerate. Amongst the most impressive pieces of labour-saving equipment available in 1840 was the horse-powered threshing machine, a device that ten years earlier had led to the notorious "Swing' riots, by which labourers sought its destruction and abolition. Progress (and we may use this word in the Victorian context, for each advance was seen as part of an on-going, almost inevitable, improvement of the lot of mankind) could not be held back, and the threshing machine was further developed with the application of steam power.

By 1853 there were 16 steam engines operating on Dorset farms. The one owned and operated by the Rev. Anthony Huxtable of Hill Farm, Sutton Waldron, was described as being of six horse power and capable of driving 'a combined threshing, straw-shaking, winnowing and sacking machine, cuts by one of Cornes' implements most of the straw into chaff, whilst the rest of the straw is propelled into a large, dry covered shed close to the cattle stalls. The same engine also is used for working two pair of mill-stones, a flour-dressing machine, a large bone mill, and a bean bruiser; and after work at night the remaining steam cooks the roots for the pigs. Above the boiler and engine is a large drying-room where the surplus heat hardens the corn for grinding. . . .'

Landowner J. J. Farquharson at Langton Long, near Blandford, had his machine designed to fill sacks with corn so that when the requisite amount was packed an automatic bell rang to inform the workers; while Mr Sturt's at Crichel, apart from its agricultural functions, was employed in sawing timber.

Whilst the landowning farmers could purchase their own expensive steam engines their tenants sought ways of obtaining the benefits without the expense. This was achieved by arrangements whereby a machine would be purchased and hired out to other farmers as and when needed. We can follow such an arrangement at Tarrant Monkton where a farmer, John Butler, formed a partnership in 1869, with William Gard, a blacksmith, in order to purchase an engine for £368, each paying half the capital cost. The farmer was the one who arranged the contacts for hiring, whilst the blacksmith looked after the mechanical side, from supplying water and fuel to providing maintenance.

Large landowners, both family and institutional, continued to dominate the landscape of Dorset and most farmers were tenants renting from them. Farm sizes varied, and were larger on the chalk

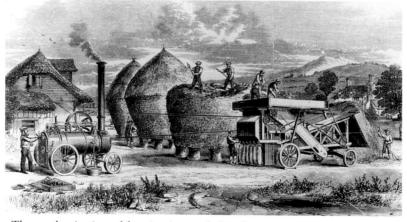

The mechanisation of farming is revealed in this engraving showing a steam driven threshing machine in operation. Work, even with these advancements, was still labour-intensive and seven labourers can be seen directly assisting in the threshing whilst the fireman controls the engine.

downlands. The process of amalgamating smaller farms continued throughout the nineteenth century. For example, in the parish of Winterborne St Martin, in 1844 the landlord, Henry Charles Sturt of Crichel, arranged the amalgamation of Clandon and Parks Farms to form a single unit of 844 acres which was leased to William Hawkins.

When Victoria became queen the Corn Laws (passed in 1815) gave protection to farmers by keeping up the price of home-grown corn by the imposition of tariffs on foreign imported corn. The Corn Laws were not popular, they kept the price of bread high and were seen by many to be against the principles of free trade. In general Dorset's landowners and farmers were in favour of the status quo but the tide in the country, particularly in the large urban and industrialised centres, was beginning to turn and the law was repealed in 1846. An anonymous correspondent, calling himself 'Oold Dorzet', writing in *The Dorset County Chronicle* acidly observes that Dorset farmers 'zess tha be all gwain to be ruand togeether – the land all gwain out o kultevashun, an the cuntry gwain to cuverd all awver wea weeds an raylroads . . . an as for the poor voke they must be all starv to deth wea vorrin corn, an beef, an poork, an a passel of thing that vree traid is gwain to bring . . . an they hav a turn me Lord Hashley out nek and krop, jist bekase he kooden zee nothin to be vrightend at.'

Lord Ashley of Wimborne St Giles, a supporter of free trade, was defeated at the 1846 election because he had supported repeal of the Corn Laws.

The economic disaster predicted by some of the Dorset farmers opposed to repeal did not materialise and farming went on in the next two decades to survive and indeed, flourish. The demand for food in the growing urban centres encouraged investment in agriculture which lead to a period known as 'High Farming'. However, the picture is not one of uniformity and some farmers, unable to find or borrow capital to invest, still found themselves struggling. The Rev. Henry Deane, farmer and vicar of Gillingham, remarked on some 'beautiful new cowsheds lately built at an expense of £300' by the Rev. Anthony Huxtable and went on to describe them as being 'very clean and totally free from the dreadful and heavy smell that most (especially ours) cowsheds possess', but Deane could only spare £100 for improvements. In 1861 he confided in a letter that 'I must have 10 more cows which will cost £150 and that I have not to spare'.

Nevertheless, in general there is a sense of well-being, as is revealed in an 1854 advertisement in *The Dorset County Chronicle*, for leasing a farm at Hillfield, near Cerne Abbas, comprising 350 acres of 'excellent Meadow, Pasture and Arable Land' to be let 'at a low Rent of £400 per annum'. The farm also boasted 'a superior stone and tiled residence, offices, and gardens, capital farm-yard, with extensive and well-arranged brick and tiled farm buildings, dairy and labourers' cottages; also, sundry enclosures of productive meadow, pasture, arable land, and orcharding, with plantation laying compact . . . the greater part recently drained and well supplied with excellent water. The tithes are commuted, and the poor rates very low. The estate is let on lease for 10 years, from Lady-day last, to Mr Thomas Stone, an opulent and highly intelligent farmer . . . '

Farmers certainly sought to improve their lot by finding better farms on the most advantageous terms, and it is sometimes surprising to see how often tenancies are changed. An example is provided by the movements of Moses Longman, who was born at Horsington in Somerset in 1800. In 1841 he was farming at Blackrow Farm, Lydlinch, but four years later had taken up a tenancy at East Farm, Owermoigne (356 acres), he remained there until 1855 when he moved to Fossil Farm, Chaldon Herring, where he had taken a 21 years' lease. He then retired from farming and went to live at Winfrith, where he died in 1883.

The agricultural depression, which began to really bite by the late 1870s, was caused primarily by the importation of cheap grain from North America and frozen meat from Argentina, Australia and New Zealand. It created real difficulties for Dorset's tenant farmers whose production costs were substantially higher than those of foreign and dominion bulk suppliers. The wheat acreage fell by almost 50 per cent, much of the arable was transformed into permanent pasture resulting in a declining value of farm rents. (Except for a short interval during World War I the consequences of this depression lasted until 1939.)

The stables at Edmondsham House, solidly constructed of brick and tile with stone dressings, bear the date 1864. Such buildings were possible because of the income derived from 'High Farming' throughout the 1850s.

An impressive brick barn, dated 1881, at Fifehead St Quentin in the Blackmore Vale. At a time of general agricultural depression dairy farmers faired best and were still able to add new buildings such as this barn.

The account of gross overcrowding in a Stourpaine cottage given by the Rev. Sidney Godolphin Osborne in 1847 formed the basis for this *Punch* cartoon, titled 'The Cottage', in which the landlord is being asked to contrast the 'excellent arrangements' in his stables with those of this family in a two-roomed cottage.

The labourers' lot was not a happy one and there were few real signs of improvement over the '60 Glorious Years' of Victoria's reign. Attention was drawn to the appalling conditions in which many labourers and their families lived by a government commission in 1843. Typical of its findings was that of a two-roomed hovel in Stourpaine where the entire family shared three beds. The father and mother shared one with two children aged four and eighteen months. Another was occupied by three daughters, and the third by the four sons. It is an example of the gross overcrowding that affected many rural communities and led to complaints about immorality which was seen as a consequence of the two sexes living in such forced proximity.

There was some improvement over the later years of the nineteenth century, due mainly to two factors, migration from the villages and the building of new cottages. A case in point is the rebuilding of Puddletown by the landowner, John Brymer, who in 1861 had purchased the estate from the 5th Earl of Orford. Here he set about the construction of a series of terraced cottages, described as 'fearsome (though sanitary)', which provided good quality and uniform housing. The first terrace was completed in 1864 to be followed by three more in 1867, 1868 and 1870, all still bearing the monogram of the landowner and the dates carved in stone shields. Whilst these factors eased the situation, we know from the Royal Commission of the Housing of the Working Class in 1884-85 that the problem had not been solved. The evidence given by Samuel Pike of Wimborne spoke of cottages being allowed to fall down so that there were fewer to accommodate the remaining families, which in turn led to severe overcrowding. In evidence he cited a cottage in Winterborne Kingston, which measured only 15 feet by 12 and provided a home for a husband, wife, their 8 children and two

Labourers' families facing eviction from their cottages in Milton Abbas in 1874. Around them are their pathetically few possessions.

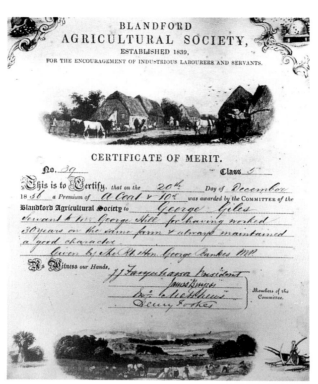

Blandford Agricultural Society awarded prizes to farm workers performing certain tasks, or for their loyalty, by issuing Certificates of Merit together with a cash prize. The illustration shows that a coat and 10 shillings were presented to George Giles in recognition of 30 years as a farm servant of George Hill. The certificate is dated 20 December 1856.

grandparents. Conditions, if possible, were even worse in the west of the county. In Nettlecombe and Powerstock many cottages were open to the rafters and thatched 'like a barn'. Many floors were of compressed earth, and access to the upper floors was by ladder only.

The low wages paid to the agricultural labourer deprived him of any opportunity to build up any form of savings, so existence was always hand-to-mouth. In testimony given by James Courtney of Corfe Castle to the magistrates in 1840 he told of his wages being 2s.

6d. a week when he worked as a youth at Snelgar's paper mill in Wareham but that more recently, as a married man with two children, he was paid £7 10s. a year by Farmer Smith of Wytch Farm. In 1846 Joseph Fowler, a farmer from Winterborne Whitechurch, had stated to the Poor Law Commissioners that 'the regular wages of the farm-labourer is 8s. a week. To the same inquiry the wife of Charles Bustle, also of Whitechurch, stated that her husband, as a carter, earned 7s. a week with a rent-free cottage, a garden and ten lugs of potato ground and, if they wanted it, a bushel of grist corn at 5s. (a lug is a square pole or perch).

The nineteenth century pattern of life for the labourer is not one of unmitigated poverty. There were improvements, not least were the rewards offered by the agricultural societies that emerged in Victorian times to unite farmers into groupings in order to more effectively pursue their agricultural activities and to provide pressure groups to further their interests. One such society was the Blandford Agricultural Society, founded in 1839, which gave certificates and cash prizes to labourers performing certain specified tasks, such as hoeing, hedging or ditching.

The idyllic impression given by this late Victorian scene of haymaking at Winterbourne Monkton shows that there were changing views of the countryside often far removed from reality.

Thomas Hardy, writing to Rider Haggard in March 1902, perhaps summarises the changes in the life of the agricultural worker in the Victorian era:

'As a child I knew by sight a Sheep Keeping boy who to my horror shortly afterwards died of want – the contents of his stomach at the autopsy being raw turnips only; his father's wages were six shillings a week, with about two pounds [£2] at harvest, a cottage rent free and an allowance of thorn faggots from the hedges as fuel . . . '

But he continues with a description of their 'present life' which is, 'almost without exception one of comfort if the most ordinary thrift be observed. I could take you to a cottage of a shepherd not many miles from here that has brass rods and carpet on the staircase, and from the open door of which you hear a piano strumming within . . . another labourer I know takes dancing lessons at a quadrille class in our neighbouring town.'

# INDUSTRIES, TRADES AND CRAFTS

Much of Dorset's industrial activity was related to agriculture, but not all. The largest and most important other industry was quarrying, which was carried on in several places but most profitably and on the largest scale at Portland and Purbeck.

Purbeck had a long established tradition of quarrying dating back to the middle ages and beyond. It expanded greatly in the Victorian period, though retaining the traditional and well-established techniques and tools of earlier times. The increased volume of stone was largely quarried by established families working small private quarries in the manner that had been adopted centuries earlier. Purbeck did not lend itself to the application of new technology as the old method of mining from underground galleries, rather than opencast, still dominated. At the head of the mines horse-powered capstans or windlasses continued to draw the stone blocks to the worksheds for shaping and dressing. The Inspector of Mines for the

Brannon's engravings accurately illustrate the Purbeck quarrying methods. On the left a block of stone is winched up by a horse-powered capstan. The other illustration shows the mining method favoured in Purbeck as the most economical way of exploiting the seams of good quality stone.

West of England, Dr C. le Neve Foster, in 1877 recorded that in Purbeck over 14,000 tons of stone had been quarried and of that almost 12,000 tons dressed for use. Frank Burt in 1893 told a visiting geologist that there were 200 men employed in 50 quarries and that there were 'from 45 to 50 quarryowners in the Isle, mostly labouring men, or skilled artisans; thus a different owner for each quarry'. Swanage was the main centre from which the stone was exported and large piles of stone, called bankers, were created along the shoreline, in readiness to be loaded on ships in the bay. C.E. Robinson writing of the 1880s, speaks of 'unsightly wharves, piled high with stone'. Even the old, over-exploited Purbeck marble quarries were re-opened for the building of the cathedral-like church at Kingston in 1874, where the architect, G.E. Street, specified its use internally for columns and decoration.

Portland was the more important source of stone in the nineteenth century and exploitation proceeded apace. The quarrying was mainly conducted on the high ground and the stone was taken by newly constructed gravity and horse-powered railways to the quays for shipment. The 1851 census recorded 480 quarrymen, 33 stonemasons, 9 stone sawyers and one 'quarry blaster', this out of a male population of 2,143 (discounting the 874 prison inmates). Steam power was introduced both to operate the cranes for lifting the stone blocks from the quarries and to provide power for stone cutting saws. In 1878 Benjamin Read of Nobel's Explosive Company demonstrated how 100 tons of capstone could be blasted in one go. The first steam traction engine arrived in about 1875 and served both for stone haulage, and at harvest time, for operating threshing machines. The railway from Weymouth to Portland opened in 1865 and, with later extensions and branches, provided an efficient method of transporting stone from the quarries to the mainland.

A major project utilising stone was the construction of the Portland breakwaters to create a large enclosed anchorage for the Royal Navy. Prince Albert laid the foundation stone in 1849 and the work, carried out largely by convicts accommodated in Portland Prison, was completed in 1872. This major work was associated with the construction of massive defensive works both on Portland, at the Verne Citadel, and across the harbour at the Nothe.

Portland harbour in about 1860. The small steam engine on the narrow shelf of the Verne shows that work on the Citadel has started. Note the old signal station on the summit.

Work in progress on the Portland Breakwater in about 1870. The ship seen to the right of the crane is HMS *Boscawen*, one of a line of naval training ships docked at Portland.

The growing application of technology to agriculture was felt everywhere. Even in the relatively conservative county of Dorset manufacturers emerged who sought to construct and supply a range of new machinery. Firms such as Oliver Maggs of Bourton were producing horse-powered threshing machines, said to be the first in the Wessex region, but were quick to exploit the growing use of steam power and, indeed, did themselves offer an efficient steam engine for farm use. In 1870 Frank Eddison, trained and apprenticed

# OLIVER MAGGS

ENGINEER AND BOILER MAKER, MILLWRIGHT, &c.,

MANUFACTURER OF
AGRICULTURAL IMPLEMENTS OF EVERY DESCRIPTION
**PATENT PORTABLE PRIZE STEAM ENGINES.**

Oliver Maggs of Bourton were in the forefront of manufacturing steam
engines for agricultural use. This advertisement of 1858
emphasised their superior quality.

A view of the Eddison works at Dorchester in about 1885, during the brief
partnership between Frank Eddison and John Allen. The photograph clearly
reveals how important the steam engine had become in the
forty-odd years since Victoria's accession.

at the famous Fowler works in Hunslet, Leeds, moved to Mar-
tinstown to start a steam traction engine hiring business for farmers
using Fowler engines. This proved so successful that seven years later
he established a works in Dorchester and, after taking John Allen
into partnership, formed the influential Dorchester Steam Plough
Works, of which the *Dorset County Chronicle* (9 Feb. 1885) was to
note 'the works now constitute one of the largest manufactories in
the town in which sixty to seventy men are employed.'

Lott and Walne became one of the most prestigious general
engineering and ironfounding firms in Dorset with its works in
Dorchester.

Whilst small-scale brickmaking continued in a great many parishes
it was the demand of a growing population, coupled with greater
expectations as to the quality of houses, which led to several large-

A bird's-eye view of the Brownsea Pottery works showing the little railway that carried both the clay and the finished sanitary ware.

scale brickworks developing, such as at Gillingham, established in 1865. The bright red brick so characteristic of their kilns can still be seen in many places in north Dorset, perhaps most dramatically in the Baptist church in the town. Verwood, long noted for its wide range of domestic wares, was able to exploit the local clays for brickmaking on a large scale.

The clays of the Purbeck area and around Poole proved to be eminently suited to the manufacture of quality earthenware. On Brownsea Island a pottery for making sanitary wares was established in 1855 by the island's owner, Colonel Waugh and a special tramway was built around the island. Workmen's cottages were erected near the kilns. Following Waugh's spectacular bankruptcy two years later, the island's next owner, G. A. F. Cavendish Bentick, MP, invested still further in the pottery. Despite a prospectus issued in 1881 proudly announcing that the firm was the recipient of the 'First and only Prize awarded by the Sanitary Institute of Great Britain', the business was unprofitable, and finally closed in 1887. The Sandford Pottery

Works, north of Wareham, comprised not only a large brick-built factory but also a terrace of workers' cottages (still standing). The sanitary ware manufactured by George Jennings at his Parkstone pottery was shipped out to the British hospitals at Varna and Scutari during the Crimean War (1854-56).

Other industries, such as button making based on cottage methods, failed to compete against the development of mass production of industrial England. The Victorian era saw a gradual stagnation followed by a rapid decline into obscurity. It is said that the button-making machine, designed by a Mr Ashton and shown successfully at the Great Exhibition of 1851, sounded the death knell of Dorset's industry.

Crowds visited the Poole Exhibition of Works of Industry and Art held in the Guildhall in 1854. It was a provincial reflection of the Great Exhibition of 1851 and sought to promote the increasing confidence of British manufacture and its marriage to art. The engraving was made by Philip Brannon of Southampton.

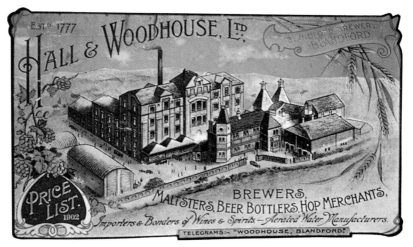

The Hall and Woodhouse Brewery at Blandford St Mary, illustrated in this 1902 price list, epitomises the style of large brewery that was being built from mid-Victorian times onwards.

The manufacture of rope, twine and netting remained throughout the Victorian period an industry of great economic importance in Bridport. Over twenty manufacturers are recorded in Hunt's Dorset Directory of 1851, including Joseph Gundry and Company which, with later amalgamations and take-overs, continues to the present time. Locally grown flax was processed in mills situated along the River Brit, most notably at Pymore, and provided much of the raw material for the various factories.

Brewing saw changes with the amalgamation of some of the old-established small breweries, such as Charles Hall's at Ansty, founded in 1777, with that of Woodhouse in Blandford. Marriage united the two families in 1847, and in 1882, they purchased John Hector and Company of Blandford, owners of a number of licensed premises. The joint venture was then based in purpose-built premises at Blandford St Mary which became known as Hall and Woodhouse, leaving a legacy which continues into the present. The consumption of ales, beers and porters by a growing population and the increased improvement in transporting them augured well for the industry. Another large brewery to be established was that of Eldridge Pope in

Dorchester, initially by purchasing the old-established Green Dragon Brewery operated by Charles Eldridge and Alfred Mason. The large brick-built brewery, opened in 1881 and soon brewing 40,000 barrels of beer a year, stands today as a monument to Victorian optimism and technical prowess.

Another famous brewery, that of the Flowers brothers of Fontmell Magna, belongs to the late Victorian period. The important contribution made by the Flowers derived from their interest in engineering, which enabled them to establish workshops to build machinery for the brewing industry throughout the country.

# TRADE AND COMMERCE

Probably the greatest change that occurred during Victoria's reign was the gradual, but accelerating, move from locally manufactured products to mass produced items for general consumption. The growing industrialisation of the country, coupled with improved maritime and rail communications, meant that a far wider and more varied range of goods became much more available, even in remote villages.

The postal services took great strides in the Victorian period, especially after the introduction of the adhesive postage stamp in 1840 and the pillar box a few years later. Indeed, Dorset has to this day what is claimed to be the oldest operational pillar box in England, situated at Barnes Cross. It is hexagonal in shape, has a vertical letter slot and dates to 1856.

Before envelopes were invented addresses were written on
the back of letters which were then folded and sealed.
This example, from 1842, addressed to James Frampton
of Moreton, shows such a letter with an unperforated 1d.
brown stamp and the Shaftesbury postmark.

East Street in Wimborne decorated with flags and foliage to commemorate
Queen Victoria's Golden Jubilee in 1897. Although the townspeople are
clearly posed for the photographer it nevertheless strongly evokes the sense
of life in a Dorset country town in the late nineteenth century.

Dorset's market towns increasingly developed shops and with the
advent of gas lighting, a real extension was possible to opening
hours, especially in the darker winter months.

Some degree of mechanisation was brought to such diverse
activities as bakeries and laundries as a consequence of which home
baking and laundering gradually declined. For example, we find a
visitor to Burden and Sons in Poole High Street in 1897 expressing
delight over the 'mysteries of coffee roasting, tea blending and the
workings of the Model Steam Bakery'. 'Machine-made' and 'hygenic'
were two terms that by the 1880s were becoming synonymous with
quality and the good life.

The local newspapers, many of which had their origins in the
mid- or late eighteenth century, blossomed not only with news but
with copious advertisements declaiming on the merits of the many
products on offer in local shops and emporia. Exotic imported goods
shared shelf space with still important local produce, even as late as

Beach and Company's chemist shop in Bridport, formerly the premises of Dr Roberts, maker of 'The Poor Man's Friend' patent medicine.

1900 Dingley and Sons of Sherborne proudly announced they were 'Agents for the Celebrated Sherborne-made Silks, as patronised by H.M. Queen Victoria, H.R.H. Princess of Wales, etc. etc.'. Hall and Son of Wimborne, established in 1836, declared they were 'Agents for Dr Jaeger's Sanitary Clothing'. J.H. Harper, hair dresser, wig maker and perfumer, situated on the Esplanade at Weymouth proudly drew attention to the fact that he was an importer of 'French and Italian Essences'.

Chemists, doctors and dentists provided health care on a private basis for those who could afford it. The Poor Law guardians could arrange for treatment, usually in the workhouses or hospitals, for only those too poor to be able to pay. Hospitals became universal during the period, most being charitable foundations and most making special provision for the poor. Patent medicines were advertised widely in newspapers, journals, trade directories and guide books. Most of the provincial chemist shops carried a range of these 'cures'. Dorset chemists were not behind when it came to promoting their own medicines: perhaps the most famous was 'The Poor Man's Friend', invented by Dr Roberts and manufactured by Beach and Barnicott of Bridport. Its claims were astonishing, including an 'unfailing remedy for wounds of every description, a certain cure for ulcerated sore legs (even if of twenty years' standing), cuts, burns, scalds, bruises, chilblains, scorbutic eruptions, and pimples on the face, sore and inflamed eyes, sore heads, cancerous tumours, etc.' The same chemists also sold 'Medicated Gingerbread Nuts. A Safe, Pleasant and Effectual Remedy for Worms'. Thomas Barling of Weymouth promoted his own dentifrice which stopped tooth decay, prevented the accumulation of tartar and hardened the gums: he also supplied, for 1s. a box, Antibilious pills, 'suitable for both sexes'.

# COMMUNICATIONS

There can be little doubt that the most important economic and social event in Victorian Dorset was the coming of the railways. Hardy, in an aside, was aware of what seemed to him the inevitable dominance of the network when he wrote, 'Flintcombe-Ash being in the middle of the cretaceous tableland over which no railway had climbed as yet . . . ' (*Tess of the d'Urbervilles*).

In 1844 Charles Castleman, a Wimborne solicitor, proposed a railway line to run from Southampton, through southern Dorset, to Exeter. The first phase of the plan was a circuitous route, through sparsely populated country, from Southampton to Dorchester. Financial backing was forthcoming, much, no doubt on the basis of an eventual link with Exeter, and the line was opened in June 1847. It arrived at the Dorset county boundary at Ashley Heath and proceeded westwards to Wimborne, then south-west to Wareham and so along the River Frome to Dorchester, where a terminus was constructed with the unfinished lines pointing due west.

This new form of rapid transport was responsible for the decline of Dorset's last major turnpike road which had been constructed in 1841-42 to link Wimborne more directly with Dorchester. Promotion and construction costs were largely met by J.W.S Sawbridge Erle Drax of Charborough who was said, by the clerk of the turnpike trustees, to have lost, in capital and interest, about £48,000, and whose sole legacy is the long wall, with its fine gates, alongside the A35.

The sixteen main turnpike roads which had been established successively since 1752 served Dorset well. In the early years of Victoria's reign they had led to a marked improvement in communication, but they could not compete with the speed and efficiency of the railways. Others followed the first: the main north-south route running from Yeovil to Weymouth was opened in

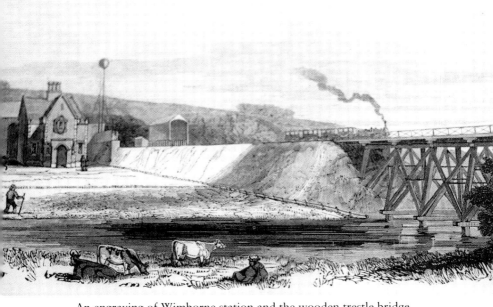

An engraving of Wimborne station and the wooden trestle bridge
over the River Stour which appeared in *The Illustrated London News*
to commemorate the opening of the Southampton
and Dorchester Railway in June 1847.

1857, to be followed by the Salisbury to Exeter line two years later,
which served both Gillingham and Sherborne. All these railways
were initiated outside Dorset and sought, while serving Dorset, to
link places beyond the county boundary; the one truly local line was
the Dorset Central Railway which ran along the Stour valley from
Wimborne to Blandford and, later, to Stalbridge to join with the
Somerset Central Railway. This became the famous Somerset and
Dorset Joint Railway and was opened throughout in 1863.

The railway network enabled farmers to obtain machinery, ferti-
lisers and animal foodstuffs easily from any part of the kingdom,
clearly reflected in the establishment of depots at most railway
stations. James Symes of Wimborne, in a trade directory for 1874-
75, announced that he was the agent in Wimborne for 'Messrs A.W.
Hall & Co's justly celebrated Artificial Manures, Nitrate of Soda,
Potato Manures, Grass Manures, Superphosphate of Lime, Wheat,
Barley and Oat Manures, Dissolved Bones.' His stores were described

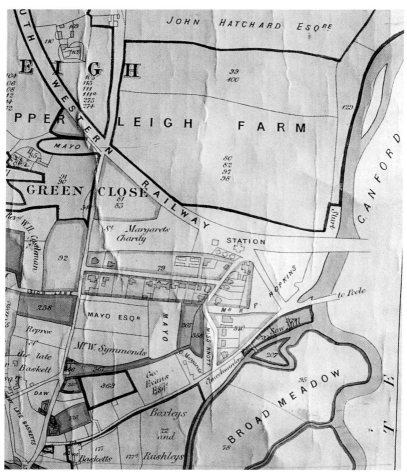

*Above* Part of the Hanham estate map of 1873 clearly showing the route
of the Southampton and Dorchester Railway into Wimborne and
the housing development which its arrival had encouraged
around the station. The Stour runs almost vertically down
the right hand side of the map.
*Opposite page* An early photograph taken around 1865 of the
Hillbutts Turnpike tollhouse in Wimborne. Behind the tollhouse
may be seen the roof of St Leonard's chapel, belonging to the
historic almshouses. The old turnpike road to Blandford
bears away to the left.

as 'close to the Wimborne Railway Station'. In the same way farmers were more easily able to market produce and stock by using the railway network and the speed of trains meant that fresh milk could be shipped in churns to large urban centres for distribution by local dairy firms such Trent's Royal Farm Dairy, '(Under Medical Supervision)', of Bournemouth. At Sturminster Marshall (Bailey Gate), on the Somerset and Dorset Railway, an important milk, butter and cheese processing works with its own sidings was established. The milk was collected from local farms by horse and cart and conveyed in 12-gallon churns to the factory for processing and shipment to its destination by rail.

The expanding railway service throughout much of Dorset in the last half of the nineteenth century opened up for the general public a rapid and relatively cheap form of regular and reliable transport. Return visits to towns such as Bath, Exeter, Salisbury and Southampton became possible in a single day, widening cultural horizons. Seaside resorts such as Weymouth (from 1857) and Swanage (after 1888) fell within the orbit of people living a hundred miles and more away.

When in 1867 the poet, William Allingham, travelled second class with Alfred, Lord Tennyson, from Lymington to Dorchester he noted in his diary: 'In our carriage a cockney Clock-winder, who gets out at every station to regulate the Railway Company's clock.'

# MILITARY

The Victorian era saw the growth and consolidation of the British Empire. Many Dorset men fought in actions and served in the outposts of empire during the nineteenth century. At various times, either in a police-keeping role or just as a symbol of the mother country, the Dorset Regiment was stationed variously in Ireland, Gibraltar, Canada, Bermuda and India. It was engaged in the Crimean War and, at the end of the century, in the South African (Boer) Wars.

Many personal anecdotes highlight the involvement of Dorset people with military events around the world as is brought home by a memorial in Fontmell Magna. It was erected to the memory of Lieut. Salkeld of the Royal Engineers who was killed in the Indian Mutiny in 1857 whilst engaged in an action to blow up the Cashmere Gate for which he was awarded the Victoria Cross. A rather different tragedy was the murder in 1861 of a veteran of the First Sikh War, Capt. John Hanham, together with his colonel, by a private at Preston Barracks. His body was brought back to Wimborne to be interred in the new cemetery. In the Borough Gardens at Dorchester is a memorial to those who served in the Tirah Expeditionary Force in 1897-98.

The Marabout Barracks, erected just to the west of Dorchester in 1795, had the great keep-like gatehouse added in 1879 and the military presence in the town confirmed for the remainder of the queen's reign.

*Opposite page top* Soldiers on parade in Poundbury Barracks, Dorchester, on 17 May 1866, when Mrs Bingham, the wife of the colonel commanding the Dorset Militia, received a presentation for her social work.
*Opposite page bottom* A view of the Marabout Barracks in Dorchester. The substantial buildings are characteristic of military establishments constructed in the Victorian era.

# WATER SUPPLIES AND SANITATION

Public health became a major concern in Victorian times, and great strides were made in the development and improvement of public utilities. The increasing density of the towns (Weymouth's population rose from under 8,000 to nearly 20,000 during the queen's reign) put enormous pressure on both the provision of clean water and disposal of effluent. It is therefore perhaps surprising to see how reluctant the various town boards were in implementing efficient sewage disposal works.

It is now difficult to imagine the depths to which many towns had sunk in the matter of sewage disposal. A letter written to *The Dorset County Chronicle* in the summer of 1846 truly reflects the problem: 'I wish particularly to draw your notice to the disgusting state of the sewers in Weymouth – the stench from the open sewers in St Mary Street, St Thomas Street and the entrance from that beautiful drive to the Smallmouth Sands, is intolerable. At a time when Weymouth is crowded with company, a nuisance so dangerous to health ought immediately to be remedied.'

It is perhaps surprising that the county town, Dorchester, remained on cesspool drainage throughout the Victorian period only obtaining its first sewerage system in 1904, almost four years after the queen's death. Indeed, its inability to effectively control the disposal of untreated sewage was held to be responsible for cholera outbreaks in Fordington in 1849 and again in 1854 when 24 victims died. As a consequence of Fordington's appalling overcrowding in slum tenements its rector, the Rev. Henry Moule (1801-80) wrote a series of letters, giving graphic details, to Prince Albert, who was Lord Warden of the Duchy of Cornwall, which owned Fordington.

Wimborne was also plagued with prevarication over the matter of putting in sewage disposal provisions. The Board of Guardians, a body with overall control of public affairs in the town, seemed

Fordington, lying to the east and adjacent to Dorchester, had become an unsavoury slum by the mid-nineteenth century. This photograph, taken in Mill Street, gives a sense of the overcrowding in tightly packed cottage terraces jammed between the River Frome and the mill leat.

incapable of reaching a decision, forcing the Home Office to intervene and arrange for drainage in West Street and from the Coach and Horses Inn into the River Stour. The work was piecemeal and ineffective, and in a seemingly retrograde step, the water closets of the workhouse were even converted back to earth closets in 1878.

In reality the argument as to whether it was preferable for untreated sewage to be poured into the county's rivers or whether earth closets provided a more satisfactory solution was much disputed: in rural areas earth closets were favoured. A report by the Medical Officer of Health to Cranborne Vestry in 1892 highlighted the dangers of untreated effluent pouring into the River Crane, 'the Board may remember some years ago an outbreak of typhoid in connection with this stream when a person living further down contracted the disease from drinking the water.' He continued, 'I would strongly recommend the exclusion of all sewage either by the substitution of earth closets or by laying down a properly constructed sewer to empty below the cottages.'

At least Sherborne seized the opportunity to create a Board of Health, as allowed under the Public Health Act of 1848, which produced a report on the sanitary conditions of the town in 1849: its conclusions painted the usual appalling picture. As a consequence a firm from Exeter was appointed to make recommendations for improvements, and between 1851 and 1855 a sewage system was installed together with piped water supplies at a cost of £7,540. This ambitious and successful scheme was financed by mortgaging the rates backed by a generous loan of £5,000 from Lord Digby of Sherborne Castle. Whilst the sewerage system was being put in place the Board ordered every house in the town to be inspected, which enabled it to demand the cleansing and whitewashing of water-closets and privies.

# THE CLERGY AND THE CHURCHES

Throughout the Victorian period the church was deeply involved in the lives of the people. The Established Anglican Church, continued to provide the 'official' religion, but Protestant non-conformity grew in influence and the Catholics, for so long persecuted, had been granted both the freedom to worship and the right to take part in public and civic life by an Act of 1829.

Dorset had only returned to the diocese of Salisbury in 1836 after a lapse of nearly 300 years. A number of notable clergy emerged during Victoria's reign. Perhaps, the one most remembered today is William Barnes (1801-82) who was not only a noted and highly regarded poet but also a schoolmaster of some distinction. Amongst

This portrait of the Rev. William Barnes (1801-86) by G. Stuckey captures something of his intensity and scholarly demeanour.

The Rev. Sidney Goldolphin Osborne (1808-89), an
Evangelical and Christian Socialist clergyman who was
vicar of Stourpaine-cum-Durweston.

the more famous of his pupils was Frederick Treves (1853-1923),
later to become a distinguished surgeon and author of many books,
including *The Highways and Byways of Dorset*.

Another notable clergyman was the Rev. Sydney Godolphin
Osborne (1808-89) who was nominated to the living at Durweston
by Lord Portman in 1841. He was soon to respond to the dreadful
living conditions of the agricultural labourers in his own parish and
that of adjoining Stourpaine by writing letters to the press, first
locally and then to *The Times*, to draw wider attention to the plight
of these people and their families. His actions so incensed the
County Tory MP, George Bankes, that he raised the matter in the

Commons. However, Lord Ashley, another of the county's MPs, and of a different complexion to Bankes, backed 'SGO', as he became known through his correspondence, and helped him found The Society for Improving the Condition of the Labouring Classes. Godolphin was committed to the principle that the Church should take a much stronger stand in trying to address social concerns and he believed his duty was to 'preach the plain truth boldly, that God will not have the poor oppressed in body or in soul'. It is not therefore surprising to find him a supporter of both Evangelicalism and Christian Socialism.

The rector of Bloxworth, the Rev. Octavius Pickard-Cambridge (1828-1917) was cast in a different mould. A natural historian of distinction he published almost 80 scientific papers on spiders alone, culminating in his authoritative, *Spiders of Dorset* (1879-81). But his interests ranged far and wide and he corresponded with scientists all over the world. He was elected a Fellow of the Royal Society in 1887, a great honour for an amateur who was also an active and dedicated pastor to his flock.

Dorset was blessed with many notable, and some outstanding clergymen, many serving their parishes for long periods. The Rev. Henry Deane (1799-1882) was vicar of Gillingham for 50 years from 1832 to 1882. His wife, Jane, who died aged 38 in 1849, kept a diary during her short marriage which provides an insight into the life of a Victorian vicar in a large rural parish. Frustrated with what she saw as her domestic inadequacies she confided to her diary in January 1839, 'Harry seems vexed that I do not attend more to household matters. I must for the future try to do this. The difficulty is how to find the time. Directly after breakfast at 8 I have Jenny to teach, Baby [Ellen Mary] to feed, and if fine to walk out with them till 11. Then I usually paint till 1. In future at 11 I will go all over the house and try to manage things better. I wish I had been born with the bump of order'. Sadly in 1843, Jenny was to die of scarlet fever, that so often incurable scourge of Victorian childhood.

The Rev. Anthony Huxtable (1808-83), another notable clergyman, was active in the pursuit of agricultural improvement. His living was in Sutton Waldron where he leased two farms from the Sturts of Crichel. He was one of the founder members of the

Blandford Agricultural Society and author of several papers on agricultural methods. He was also a dedicated churchman, of High Church or Tractarian persuasion, who founded the Blandford Clerical Society, which continues to the present day.

Much as Henry Deane had raised money, including £550 from his own resources, to rebuild the greater part of Gillingham parish church, so Huxtable, largely with his wife's money, completely rebuilt St Bartholomew's church at Sutton Waldron. With its graceful spire it stands today as a monument to him and as an example of the enthusiasm for rebuilding, refurbishing and building churches throughout Dorset during the span of Victoria's reign.

Many of Dorset's medieval churches, despite occasional repairs and more frequent additions, were often ill-kempt and dilapidated and not at all in keeping with the new Anglican enthusiasms. Today, many regret the fervour with which the Victorians 'tidied up' ancient churches. But the landowners and clergy of the time were keen to see churches refurbished or rebuilt in styles that reflected the rediscovered mystery of religious worship. The church should be fit to be a house of God and inspiration came from the great churches of Gothic England.

This view may be summed up in a letter written by the Rev. Nathaniel Bond of Creech Grange to Joseph Weld of Lulworth in November 1858: 'It has occurred to me, whether in the proposed repairs to the church at Coombe Keynes, it might not be best, and in the end the cheapest plan, to pull down the whole structure, including the Tower and the Chancel, and rebuild it on a reduced scale, substituting a small Bell Turret for the present dilapidated Tower.'

What is perhaps surprising is that Dorset supplied many local architects for designing its churches, including Christchurch born Benjamin Ferrey (1810-80) who, after schooling at Wimborne Grammar School, trained under A.W.N. Pugin. Amongst his churches are Melplash, for which he chose the Norman style, built in 1845-6, Osmington, in the Perpendicular style in 1846, Plush in 1848 and All Saints, with its towering spire, in Dorchester in 1843-5, described by Pevsner as 'Faultless Second Pointed'. John Hicks (1815-69) of Dorchester had an active practice and was responsible for a number of designs, mainly it must be said restorations. Thomas Hardy was

The soaring tower of Cattistock church, designed by George Gilbert Scott
and built in 1874, is described by Sir Nikolaus Pevsner as 'original, bold,
brilliant and decidedly Late Victorian'. It certainly dominates his father's
church buildings erected 17 years earlier.

articled to Hicks in 1856 and, whilst working under his tutelage, was no doubt responsible for numerous contributions. It is known that the drawings for the church of St Martin at Shipton Gorge, built 1861-2, were by him. His work for Hicks, and later G.R. Crickmay, who took over Hicks's practice in 1869, left him with an abiding interest and concern for church restoration which he pursued intermittently long after becoming a great author and poet.

Probably the two most important churches architecturally are St James at Kingston, financed by Lord Eldon and built to the designs of G.E. Street in 1880, and George Gilbert Scott's Cattistock built in 1857, with its outstanding tower added by his son in 1874. Pugin himself designed Halstock church and, more significantly, added the great colourful stained glass window in the south transept at Milton Abbey.

The Non-conformists also extended their influence. By 1851 there were 147 Methodist places of worship in the county with places for

*Above* On Bere Heath stands this small Wesleyan Methodist chapel, a reminder of the small scale but widespread influence of Methodism in rural Dorset. It was opened in 1850.
*Opposite* This aerial photograph of Kingston shows the large scale and dominant position of G.E. Street's cathedral-like church built in 1873-80 for the third Earl of Eldon. In the foreground, and much more parochial in scale, stands Kingston's 1833 church designed by G.S. Repton.

The great stone gothic-styled Wesleyan Methodist
church in Gillingham was built in 1872 and had an
integral manse and school rooms.

18,000 people. By mid-century it has been estimated that 'one person in 15 or 16 attended a Methodist service on a regular basis'. The
Congregationalists or Independents had 69 chapels and the Baptists
only 15. These must be compared with the 304 churches of the
Anglicans and the mere seven of the Roman Catholics.

All but two of the Catholic churches are Victorian, of these one of
the most distinctive is that dedicated to Our Lady of Martyrs and St
Ignatius at Chideock built in 1870-2 at the expense of Charles Weld,
who also was his own architect. Poole's Catholic church was one of
the earliest, being built in 1839.

Other Protestant sects and groups were late in arriving: the Salva-
tion Army, for example, came to Wimborne in 1888.

# SCHOOLS AND ADULT EDUCATION

Education for the majority of the population in Dorset had either been non-existent or, at best, ad hoc and occasional. The long-established grammar schools such as those founded by Thomas Hardie at Dorchester, the Queen Elizabeth Grammar School at Wimborne, and Sherborne School continued to function and flourish. But during Victoria's reign this was to change dramatically, with schooling becoming universal and compulsory before she celebrated her Golden Jubilee. The Church and the Non-conformists both played a significant and seminal role in attempting to widen educational provision for children. Schooling was seen as an effective way of instilling discipline and respect for authority in the wider, previously largely untutored population: what one contemporary called, 'Moral improvement through instruction.'

Two personalities from Dorset figured prominently in the development of nineteenth century primary education. The Rev. Dr. Andrew Bell, rector of Swanage between 1801 and 1816, was a protagonist for the National Society for Promoting Education of the Poor in the Principles of the Established Church throughout England and Wales, established in 1811. Some 30 years before Victoria's accession Bell had set out his vision, 'It is not proposed that the children of the poor be educated in an expensive manner, or even taught to write and cypher . . . It may suffice to teach the generality, on an economical plan, to read their Bible and understand the doctrines of our holy religion.'

William Edward Forster, architect of universal elementary education, was born at Bradpole in 1818 into a strongly Quaker family and, on becoming a Liberal MP for Bradford (Yorks) in 1861, promoted the cause of elementary education. The legislation by which he is best remembered, the famous Forster Education Act of 1870, is one of the milestones in educational history. By establishing a national body, the School Board, it ensured that schooling became universal throughout England and Wales. Where existing Church of England National Schools existed these were absorbed into the system without sacrificing their religious independence.

An example of the growing enthusiasm for primary education comes from Puddletown where the landowner, John Brymer, financed the magnificent stone-built school which still stands and is in use today. The school opened in 1865 and was for both boys and girls. The master and mistress, George and Sarah Collins were aided by a pupil-teacher, Tryphena Sparks, a cousin of Thomas Hardy. Schooling, as elsewhere at the time was not free, and it is interesting to see how charges were graded according to the status of the parents:

Farmer: 6d. per week per child.

Tradesmen: 6d. for the first child, 4d. for the second and 2d. for the third and subsequent children.

Mechanics: 4d. for the first child, 3d. for the second and 1d. for the third and subsequent children.

Labourers: 2d. for the first two children and 1d. for the third and subsequent children.

The Non-conformists had started provision for their children's education with the foundation of the British and Foreign School Society, founded in 1814 by Joseph Lancaster. Their schools were usually constructed as part of the chapel or church in which the dissenters worshipped. In Bridport, for example, the minister found the chapel inadequate and proposed a new building, to whose chapel would be added 'commodious School-rooms in a prominent situation'. The foundation stone was laid in 1859 and the school opened the following year, but it soon proved to be too small for so Non-conformist a town as Bridport, and within a few years five additional class rooms were added.

Concern that some children were missing their education led the rector of Chettle, the Rev. John West, a former missionary in Canada, to establish in 1857 a school at Farnham for gypsy children who he felt were in need of a Christian education. The school enjoyed only a limited success and eventually closed to become the Pitt-Rivers Museum.

Well-built of good stone, with a Welsh slate roof, Puddletown School proclaims the importance of wealthy patronage turned benevolently to educating the young. It was entirely financed by the local landowner, John Brymer, and constructed in 1864-65.

The Catholics, with a much more restricted legacy of freedom of worship within the kingdom and labouring still under more than two centuries of disadvantage, also made moves to provide education for their children. In 1843, a prominent landowner of Marnhull, Mr Hussey, 'gave a valuable piece of land in perpetuity to build a school room, and cottage and garden for a Teacher'. By 1846 the school had been built and Mr Hussey endowed it with £20 a year for upkeep and the teacher's salary. Within 20 years the school was seen to be too small for its potential attendance and in 1868 additions were made under the supervision of the Rev. Father Thomas Spencer. Forster's Education Act made a grant towards the school's costs. By the time of the 1880 Education Act, which made schooling compulsory up to the age of ten years, the Marnhull Catholic School had an attendance of around 35 pupils.

Most of the union workhouses had their own schools, as did Dorchester Prison. By 1851 the national census recorded a total of 648 day schools functioning throughout Dorset.

The provision of adult education was a significant cultural step taken in Victorian Dorset. It is often churchmen who were in the forefront of developing this facility for an ill-educated, working population. A poster of 1858 promoting an evening school at Cranborne contained the following comment: 'The Vicar of Cranborne has great satisfaction in stating that the behaviour of the Evening Scholars last winter was most encouraging and the young men of Cranborne are again earnestly recommended to avail themselves of the advantages which the Evening School offers for the improvement of their minds. They will thus, by God's Grace, be preserved from many temptations to evil, to which they might otherwise be exposed, and an improved education may be the means of advancing their temporal welfare.'

The founding of institutes and reading rooms in towns and villages provided centres for lending libraries and lecture rooms. Even as early as 1851 there were institutes in Blandford, Bridport, Poole,

Sherborne Boys School viewed from the north as depicted in *The Illustrated London News* in 1861 showing the many extensions made in the early Victorian period; a time which saw it become a major public school.

MOWLEM INSTITUTE.

This Building was erected by JOHN MOWLEM ESQ[RE].
A NATIVE OF SWANAGE,
founder of the Firm of JOHN MOWLEM & C[o] of LONDON
and was presented to the PARISH of SWANAGE
on the 19th DAY of JANUARY 1863
together with the sum of £200-3 per cent CONSOLS,
for REPAIRS and INSURANCE,
the BUILDING to be used for the benefit and
mutual improvement of the working classes;
and for lecturing mechanical and other scientific
instruction and intellectual improvement generally,
not excluding occasional meetings
ON FREE MASONRY.

K. BROOKING
BUILDER.

G.R. CRICKMAY
ARCHITECT.

John Mowlem returned to his birth place of Swanage in 1845 at the age of 57. From the wealth he had accumulated through his construction business he made many endowments including the Mowlem Institute, which was for intellectual improvement. It characterises the high moral and educational ideals so much part of the cultural life of Victorian England.

Sherborne, Sturminster Newton and Wareham, each with a library ranging from the 158 books in Sherborne to 1000 in both Poole and Bridport (today the Bridport Institute is still the library). Lectures were held on a regular basis on such topics as astronomy, literature, the fine arts and zoology. Interestingly, at Blandford it was 'On any subject, excepting Religion and Politics'. Small subscriptions were levied to belong to these institutions, thus in Bridport its ordinary working men paid 2d. a week.

A more articulate and educated public was soon demanding access to books. A number of benfactors, such as J.J. Norton of Poole, responded by providing free public libraries. That at Poole was opened in 1887 to commemorate Queen Victoria's Golden Jubilee.

William Barnes spoke regularly at a number of these institutes and lectured in villages throughout the county. The arrival of the railway network made this enterprise possible, and his daughter, Laura, noted in her diary in 1861 that her father had packed his over night bag for a lecture tour embracing, 'Tonight at Wimborne, tomorrow Blandford, Wednesday at Salisbury, Thursday at Shaftesbury, Friday at Mere, our first home'.

Generally, the Victorian era was one of increasing interest and concern in the historic environment, and the study of archaeology became much more rigorous under the disciplines imposed by Augustus Pitt-Rivers (1827-1900); this was coupled with the desire to display and explain the past to the wider public and was enshrined in the provision of a museum. The Dorset County Museum was established in 1845, and some thirty years later the Dorset Natural History and Antiquarian Field Club was founded at Sherborne, but was later amalgamated with the County Museum.

A notable exponent of the growing interest in antiquarianism was the Dorset born Charles Warne (1801-87), who in 1872 published the first authoritative popular account in his *Ancient Dorset: The Celtic, Roman, Saxon and Danish Antiquities*.

The Victorian period was one of great strides in education borne of an increasing recognition of the importance of literacy and numeracy, especially as work became more technical and increasing legislation affecting people's lives needed to be explained. National newspapers and the expansion of the local press meant that those unable to read were seriously deprived of information that might be not only interesting but of direct importance to their lives.

# CULTURAL LIFE AND LEISURE

Improved education, though quite basic, enabled people to find more profitable work as better employment opportunities opened up. In general terms, despite continuing and severe poverty, a greater number of an increasing population found themselves better off, often with a little surplus money. It must be remarked that a great deal was still spent in inns and alehouses, drunkenness remaining a scourge throughout the nineteenth century. Most taverns did offer entertainment and, for working men, provided a 'club' in which they could engage in a number of games and some gambling. The Temperance Movement attempted to lure people away from public houses by offering similar facilities and non-alcoholic beverages, but they had very limited and, ultimately, declining success. One founded in 1855 by Thomas Horlock Bastard (1796-1898) at Charlton Marshall as a working men's club provided a library of 700 books but did not permit smoking or the drinking of alcohol.

The introduction of statutory Bank Holidays in 1871 had the effect of changing the ethos of providing leisure for working people. Holidays had become ad hoc in the earlier nineteenth century and were much tied in with post-harvest celebrations and the arrival of fairs at market towns. The Bank Holidays and the increasing provision of free Saturday afternoons gave more leisure time. Days at the seaside became popular and Weymouth, with its railway connection forged in 1857, began to attract increasing numbers of day trippers. The corporation provided shelters overlooking the wide sands of Weymouth's renowned strand and private enterprise soon laid on seaside shows and donkey rides, whilst the hurdy-gurdy, with its marmoset monkey, was a feature of the Esplanade. Victorian children, with large-brimmed hats to protect them from the sun's rays, crowded along the shore enjoying the Victorian passion for sea-blown 'ozone'.

For the middle class the opportunity for a holiday of several days became feasible and small hotels and boarding houses were soon catering for families. Journeys into the countryside surrounding Weymouth and, especially, to Portland became *de rigeur* for all visitors staying more than a day or two. Paddle steamers offered the chance to put to sea and visits to Torquay or the Isle of Wight provided a new sensation for the passengers – most of whom had been no further out to sea than the pier head. Less welcome for 194 passengers on the PS *Bournemouth* was its running on to the rocks at Portland, at full speed and in thick fog, in August 1886. Fortunately, no lives were lost, although the vessel became a total wreck.

Sir Henry Edwards, MP for Weymouth, financed the lofty, cast-iron clock tower, with its large gilded relief of the Queen's head, which still dominates the Esplanade, as the borough's commemoration of Queen Victoria's Golden Jubilee in 1887. After her death

*Above* A watercolour painting of the wrecked steamer *Bournemouth* which, with 194 passengers, struck the rocks off Portland in August 1886.
*Opposite page top* The popularity of the seaside watering place knew no bounds. With easy railway connections and the advent of paid Bank Holidays the resorts became crowded, as can be seen in this view of Weymouth beach in 1900.
*Opposite page bottom* Swanage, renowned for its stone, capitalised on the enthusiasm for sea bathing by becoming a resort. In this photograph the wide expanse of gently sloping beach is very evident.

Cricket being played in the grounds of Canford Manor in about 1850.

in 1901 a statue to her was erected at the northern end of the Esplanade, allowing her to gaze towards that of her grandfather at the southern end.

Swanage also benefited from the enthusiasm for seaside pleasures. After the arrival of the branch railway in 1888, it developed quite rapidly, but was never able to vie with its larger neighbours to east and west. A pier was constructed to the south of the town which enabled passengers to embark on the paddle steamers that provided a regular service to the much larger and faster-growing resort of Bournemouth.

Dorset never entered the county cricket league nor did any of its towns boast nationally famous league football teams, but both games were represented in town and village. Cricket, especially, was a popular game played throughout the county by enthusiastic amateur teams. By the beginning of the 1884 season, following a meeting earlier in the year in Wimborne, The South Hants and Dorset Football Association was formed offering membership to any teams playing within a 50 miles radius of Wimborne 'in either of the two counties'. This encouraged the adoption of team colours: those of Blandford were described as being a 'claret coloured jersey, with vertical orange stripe, claret and orange cap, with white knicks'. Local loyalties and enthusiasms led occasionally to unruly behaviour. In the Hants and Dorset Junior Cup final played between Poole Rovers and Cowes at Wareham in March 1887 the Poole supporters were accused of threatening 'the Cowes team with personal violence, both before and after the match, and pelted some of the players during the time of play with stones, besides using the most abusive language'.

Bicycling became popular in the late 1870s and clubs were founded in many centres. These were to provide competitions which included both long hauls and racing. The Poole club was formed in 1878 and had an entrance fee of 5s. A year later Wimborne created a club with the title of Wandering Minstrels, the rather sombre uniform

The well laid out Dorchester Borough Gardens, with winding paths, fountain and bandstand, characterise the rise in the provision of public pleasure grounds. This photograph was taken in 1898.

The pleasure grounds of Poole Park in the summer of 1900.

consisted of black polo cap, black coat, shepherd's plaid knicks, black stockings and a black and white tie. Their headquarters were at Tapper's Railway Hotel.

Corporations in the towns soon regarded the provision of recreational space as an important part of their civic responsibility. These usually made provision for the playing of sports such as tennis and other ball games and, for the more sedentary folk, had walks adorned with flower beds surrounded by lawns (usually with notices stating 'Keep off the Grass') with frequent park benches, some under shelter. Weymouth was quick to establish pleasure grounds, the Alexandra Gardens providing flower-lined walks for residents and visitors to amble at leisure, although the privilege cost them one penny. The land for the laying out of Dorchester's pleasure grounds was purchased by the corporation in 1885. Puddletown landowner and county MP, Colonel William Brymer, presented the bandstand in time for the formal opening in July 1896. Poole Corporation had been considering the provision of public gardens and pleasure grounds since 1885 and were delighted to accept the generous free gift by Lord Wimborne of land running along the shores of Parkstone Bay. The park was formally opened in 1890 by the Prince of Wales, accompanied by the Princess of Wales.

# CRIME AND PUNISHMENT

The Victorian era saw considerable changes in the severity of both sentencing and punishment though the harsh treatment of convicts continued.

The number of capital offences, which had encompassed crimes ranging from theft and sheep-stealing to murder, were gradually reduced in number. Public executions were the norm in the early part of the reign (but were abolished in 1868) and William Mabey of Sutton Poyntz recorded that in 1863 'two men were hung in

Dorchester, as the county town, contained the prison. This view shows the Victorian brick buildings of 1884-45, with their Welsh slate roofs, dominating the townscape.

An engraving of Portland convicts working in the quarries producing stone for the Portland Breakwater in 1881.

Dorchester, being the last to be hanged in public. I went from Sutton to see this, staying at my cousin's house in Glyde Path Hill where from one of the bedrooms you could see everything quite clearly. I waited an hour then they were cut down and laid in their coffins. Thousands of people came from all parts to witness the hanging'. Thomas Hardy left accounts of two executions he witnessed at Dorchester gaol, the first of Martha Browne in 1856 and the second, through a large brass telescope from the heath near his home, a couple of years later.

Dorchester was the assize town and home of the county gaol. The Quarter Sessions rotated around the county and took place in several of the market towns. The punishments handed down were often severe. At the Easter Sessions in 1872 a labourer, Christopher Hunt, was found guilty of stealing three fowls and a sack bag, for which theft he received seven years penal servitude and seven years police supervision. The rare survival of a letter from an educated and articulate vagrant, George Atkins Brine, casts much light on attitudes towards punishment in 1847. He wrote from Dorchester Gaol, 'I am committed for trial at the sessions on a charge of vagrancy for being found asleep in a stall belonging to Mark Sherrin the butcher. I expect a term of imprisonment and a corporal punishment by flagellation'. Of the magistrate who dealt with his case at the Petty Sessions he wrote, 'It seems a pleasure to him to vomit his waspish and dyspeptic spleen at me'. At the Epiphany Sessions Brine was sentenced to three months hard labour, during which time he was to be punished by whipping. Corporal punishment continued to be used throughout the Victorian period but its application was limited in 1898.

The most famous prison was that built on Portland in 1848-50. It had two roles, one was to provide labour for the construction of the Breakwater and the other was as an experiment in dealing with prisoners who had been sentenced to transportation to New South Wales: a punishment which was halted in 1840 and abolished in 1857.

# ARISTOCRACY AND GENTRY

Throughout the nineteenth century most landownership in Dorset was confined to relatively few wealthy families. There were a number of great houses, some of antiquity, which were the homes of aristocratic or landed families. In the Return of the Owners of Land, made to Parliament between 1874 and 1876, it was shown that there were 3,409 owners of more than one acre of Dorset and between them they owned 571,757 acres. Dorset's largest landowner was the pioneering archaeologist Major General Augustus Lane Fox-Pitt-Rivers with an estate of 24,942 acres centred on his house at Rushmore on Cranborne Chase. The gross annual rental value of his land brought in £33,682. Sherborne Castle was the home of the second largest landowner, George Digby Wingfield-Digby, who held 21,230 acres with a gross annual rental value of £36,106. The Earl of Ilchester, with large holdings in Abbotsbury and around Melbury Osmond, held close to 16,000 acres. Kingston Lacy and Corfe Castle provided the main holdings of Walter Ralph Bankes, amounting to over 19,000 acres with a valuation of nearly £15,000. The other great landowners included the Earl of Shaftesbury at Wimborne St Giles, the Earl of Eldon at Corfe Castle (Kingston), Lord Portman at Bryanston, the Welds of East Lulworth, the Sturts of Crichel, the Guests of Canford, the Sheridans of Frampton. Aristocrats such as the Marquis of Salisbury, with a manor house at Cranborne, owned smaller but still significant estates, the Marchioness of Westminster owned a sizeable estate centred on Motcombe and included the village of Stalbridge.

The political influence wielded by the aristocracy and gentry was very considerable. Many served at a local level as magistrates and several were MPs, some holding important offices of state. Of course, the titled landowners could sit in the House of Lords but their real influence was exercised at a more local level. When the Dorset

The unmistakably tall and straight figure of the 7th Earl of Shaftesbury (1801-88) seen in the gardens of his Dorset home, St Giles House, together with his beloved wife Minnie.

County Council was created in 1889 of the 76 elected members no less than 47 were peers, the sons of peers, esquires and gentlemen of rank.

One of the more outstanding figures was Anthony Ashley Cooper (1801-85) who was elected MP for Shaftesbury in 1826 and was to become both advocate and initiator of a number of major social reforms connected with employment in factories and mines. When he succeeded to the earldom as the 7th earl in 1851 he continued to pursue in the House of Lords the many radical reforms started when he was an MP. He was a curious and sometimes contradictory mix of attitudes and yet, throughout his life remained firm to those overriding convictions that elevate him to the rank of one of the great Englishmen. As one remarked, 'Not the least remarkable thing about Lord Shaftesbury is that, even in his own day, his virtues were allowed to far outweigh his vices'. He is, of course, commemorated by the statue of Eros in Piccadilly Circus, whose bow points directly towards Wimborne St Giles, the place of his birth and his burial.

Melbury House is a building of many periods but in 1884-85 a great
Tudor style tower was added by the 5th Earl of Ilchester. The
contrast with the original Tudor lantern tower, which may be
seen to the right, is astonishing.

Another of the notable aristocratic politicians was Edward Berkeley
Portman (1799-1888). After a distinguished academic career at
Oxford, he entered parliament as Liberal MP for the County of
Dorset in 1823. He was created Baron Portman in 1837 and from
that date played a prominent and active role in the House of Lords,
becoming a counsellor of the Duchy of Cornwall which held
extensive estates in Dorset. He was elevated to Viscount Portman in
1873. His eldest son, William Henry, dissatisfied with the Georgian
Bryanston mansion situated near the River Stour, in the late 1890s

engaged the architect Norman Shaw to construct a large 'palace' on the high ground above the river. Bryanston was the last great country house to be built in Dorset, and in many ways sums up the obsession with money and class that so shaped the Victorian age. As Sir Nikolaus Pevsner remarked, 'Everything about Bryanston proclaims the pride of the well-born and super wealthy'.

Hunting remained the abiding recreational passion for most of the landed classes and in Dorset there were several hunts. Amongst its leading proponents was James John Farquharson (1784-1871), owner of Langton House and 6,000 acres. He pursued his passion for over half a century and in 1858 was presented with a large equestrian portrait of himself dressed as Master of the Foxhounds (now in the Dorset County Museum). At the public dinner to

The great central block of Bryanston, with one of its two flanking wings. The last of the great mansions built in the county, Bryanston was completed in 1894 and it stands today as a great landmark in the chalklands of central Dorset. The architect Norman Shaw created this huge house for the 2nd Viscount Portman.

The renowned huntsman Squire Farquharson (1784-1871) on horseback.
This was the portrait presented to him at Dorchester in 1858.

The Rev. Nathaniel Bond and his family on the terrace outside Creech Grange. This fine study embraces all those qualities that were so much a feature of life for the gentry classes in Victorian Dorset.

commemorate the presentation a poem was read which opened with the following quatrain:

> *Let's up and be going, for this is the day*
> *The true hearts of Dorset must hasten away;*
> *Fox-hunters and sportsmen, and gentlemen all*
> *With hearty good will respond to the call.*

The third verse effectively encapsulates so many attitudes of mid-century, rural Dorset:

> *Great service he's done us, for so it appears,*
> *This County he's hunted for fifty good years;*
> *Well done, worthy Squire! and the motto for you*
> *Will be carried nem. con. 'Staunch, Steady and True'.*

Many of the paintings in the great houses reflect the enthusiasm for hunting, angling and shooting that made up much of the leisure time of both the ladies and gentlemen of wealth.

Not infrequently some of the mansions were rented out when, for one reason or another, the owners had to be absent. In the case of Chettle House we learn of an eminent Queen's Counsel, William Buhley Glasse, taking a lease in 1884 together with the shooting on the estate. Merley House, home of the Willett family, was leased in 1869 by William Charles Wentworth, a famous Australian, for £450 a year.

Fortunes that sustained the landowning families were sometimes from inherited wealth supplemented by the income from the rents from tenants on the estates, some came from industrial or trading enterprises. There seemed to be a sufficient economic cushion to allow the landowners to ride out the period of agricultural depression which dominated the last three decades of Victoria's reign. Only two per cent of the county's acreage was put on the market at this difficult time.

# THE VICTORIAN LEGACY

It is difficult to summarize the impact of the 63 'Glorious Years' of Victoria's reign. In expanding technology great and durable changes were made to transport, agriculture and industry, altering people's lives in a manner never seen before. A wider range of foodstuffs became available, much of foreign origin; American and Argentinian beef, bread grain from America and Canada, butter and mutton or lamb from Australia and New Zealand, wines from France, Spain and Italy and exotic fruits from both the East and West Indies. The range and availability of clothing, too, far surpassed anything existing earlier. But it was not only an upsurge in the world of material things, but also in spiritual provision, leading to the building of many new churches and chapels; often with schools associated with them. The great internecine squabbles in the Church of England drew adherents to both the Evangelical and High Church wings, facts still observable in many new or restructured Victorian churches. Yet, conversely, the Victorian era, more than any other, saw the greater secularisation of society. Civil registration superceded (though it did not displace) church registration. Church courts were wound up, wills no longer needed to be proved in ecclesiastical courts and after the 1870 Education Act non-denominational schools became available.

Great changes were brought about in administration and this eventually led to the democratisation of society. The political franchise was gradually widened through three Reform Acts (though it never included votes for women). The old quarter session system of county government was superceded by the county councils and, shortly afterwards by urban, district and parish councils all with elected members.

Yet through this period of unprecedented change there still ran conservative threads, whereby old customs and traditions were maintained, particularly in some of the more remote villages. Respect for

Thomas Hardy (1840-1928), one of the greatest of
the Victorian novelists, is seen in this photograph
as a man in his mid-forties.

authority and for the landed classes seems to have been well
maintained in Dorset throughout the nineteenth century but we can
see now that the fabric had been torn to reveal the world of the
twentieth century beyond. It is true, as Barbara Kerr remarked, 'The
villager was ready and eager to become, for better or for worse, a
townsman. By the time that machines in fields, barns and dairies
could lessen the toil of men, few were left to savour the triumph of
feeling themselves masters where formerly their lives had been bound
to the soil.'

The Victorian legacy that perhaps in the end will prove most
durable is Thomas Hardy's literature. It was his Wessex novels and
poems which brought the life of Victorian Dorset so vividly to the
eyes of the outside world. In books such as *Tess of the d'Urbervilles*
(1891) or *The Mayor of Casterbridge* (1886) descriptions of both
rural and town life are told with a perception that, surely, can only
come from a native. To him we need to turn for human insights and
a poetic understanding of Victorian Dorset.

# FURTHER READING

Ash, J., *West Stour in Dorset: A Journey Through the Centuries*, 1980

Ash, J., *Victorian Vicar: Henry Deane, Vicar of Gillingham 1832-1882*, 1982

Barnard, A., *The Noted Breweries of Great Britain*, Vol. IV, 1891

Bateman, J., *The Great Landowners of Great Britain and Northern Ireland*, 4th edition, 1883

Best, G., *Shaftesbury: a Biography of the Seventh Earl*, 1974

Bettey, J.H., *The Island and Royal Manor of Portland*, 1970
*Dorset: City and County Histories*, 1974
*Man and the Land: Farming in Dorset 1846-1996*, 1996

Bradbury, M. and Gassmann, C., *One Hundred and Fifty Years A-Growing: St Mary's School, Marnhull, from 1846 to 1996*, 1997

Brocklebank, J., *Victorian Stone Carvers in Dorset Churches, 1856-1880*, 1979

Burnett, D., *A Dorset Camera, 1855-1914*, 1974
*Dorset Shipwrecks*, 1982

Chedzoy, A., *William Barnes: a Life of the Dorset Poet*, 1985

Clegg, L., *A History of Wimborne Minster and District*, 1960
*A History of Dorchester*, 1972

Colloms, B., *Victorian Country Parsons*, 1977

Cullingford, C., *A History of Poole*, 1988

Densham, W. and Ogle, J., *The Story of the Congregational Churches of Dorset*, 1899

Draper, J., *Thomas Hardy's England*, 1984

Gourlay, A.B., *A History of Sherborne School*, 2nd edit., 1971

Hearl, T.W., *William Barnes the Schoolmaster*, 1966

Holmes, M., *Parkstone Recollections*, 1983

Hutchins, J., *The History and Antiquities of the County of Dorset*, 3rd edition, 4 vols, edited by W. Shipp and J.W. Hodson, 1861-70

Irvine, P., *Victorian and Edwardian Dorset*, 1977

Jones, I., *The Stalbridge Inheritance 1780-1854*, 1993

Kerr, B., *Bound to the Soil: A Social History of Dorset 1750-1918*, 1968

Lewer, D. (editor), *John Mowlem's Swanage Diary, 1845-1851*, 1990

Lucking, J.H., *Railways of Dorset*, 1968

Millgate, M., *Thomas Hardy*, 1982

Newman, J. and Pevsner, N., *Dorset: The Buildings of England*, 1972

Page, W. (editor), *The Victoria History of the County of Dorset,* Vol. II, 1908

Popham, H., *The Dorset Regiment,* 1970

Robinson, C.E., *A Royal Warren or Rambles in Purbeck,* 1882

Ruegg, L.H., 'Farming in Dorsetshire', *Jnl of the Royal Agricultural Society,* 15, part II, No. XXXIV (1854).

Street, R.T.C., *Victorian High-Wheelers: the Social Life of the Bicycle where Dorset meets Hampshire,* 1979

Thompson, M.W., *General Pitt-Rivers,* 1977

Ward, E., 'Archdeacon Anthony Huxtable (1808-1883) – Radical Parson, Scientist and Scientific Farmer', *Procs. DNH&AS,* Vol. 101 (1979)

Waymark, J., 'The Agricultural Depression in Dorset c.1870-1900 and the Duchy of Cornwall', *Procs. DNH&AS Vol.* 117 (1975)

# ACKNOWLEDGEMENTS

I would like to thank the Librarian and staff at the Dorset County Library, the Archivist and staff at the Dorset Record Office and the Curator and staff at the Dorset County Museum for allowing access to, and use of books, documents and other records in their respective care.

My wife, as always, deserves special thanks for her considerable help, advice and forbearance.

Some of the photographs for this book were taken by the author, but Jude James would like to thank the following for allowing the inclusion of illustrations in their possession or for which they hold the copyright. Valerie Dicker: page 65: Dorset County Museum: pages 10, 41 (top & bottom), 46, 63, 69, 72, 73, 76: Dovecote Press: pages 9 (top), 11, 12, 14, 19, 20, 21, 23, 27, 29, 37, 43, 50, 55, 56, 60 (top & bottom), 64, 71: Stuart Morris: page 25 (top): The National Portrait Gallery, London: page 45: The Priest's House Museum, Wimborne: frontispiece, page 39: Royal Commission Historical Monuments (England), © Crown Copyright: pages 9 (bottom), 34, 49, 70.

*The*

# DISCOVER DORSET

*Series of Books*

A series of paperback books providing informative illustrated
introductions to Dorset's history, culture and way of life.
The following titles have so far been published.

All the books about Dorset published by The Dovecote Press
are available in bookshops throughout the county,
or in case of difficulty direct from the publishers.
The Dovecote Press Ltd, Stanbridge,
Wimborne, Dorset BH21 4JD
Tel: 01258 840549.